BLUFF YOUR WAY IN ECONOMICS

STUART TROW

RAVETTE PUBLISHING

Published by Ravette Publishing Limited
P.O. Box 296
Horsham
West Sussex RH13 8FH

Telephone: (01403) 711443
Fax: (01403) 711554

First printed 1996
Revised 1997, reprinted 1998

Series Editor – Anne Tauté

Cover design – Jim Wire, Quantum
Printing & binding – Cox & Wyman Ltd.
Production – Oval Projects Ltd.

The Bluffer's Guides series is based
on an original idea by Peter Wolfe.

The Bluffer's Guides™, Bluffer's™
and Bluff Your Way™ are Trademarks.

An Oval Project
for Ravette Publishing.

CONTENTS

INTRODUCTION

This book is for those who positively ache to know more about economics, but have always been afraid to ask. How many times have you been at a dinner party and wished that you could say something sensible about the Bretton Woods agreement or EMU? Economics is a bluffer's delight, crammed full of obscure terms to describe the quite ordinary.

To the untrained mind, the main application of economics might seem to be to confuse those people who would otherwise think that economists don't know what they are talking about. Nothing could be further from the truth. Economics is a scientific, highly evolved subject that explains exactly what will happen in a given set of circumstances. It then provides a convincing explanation for why it didn't happen as forecast, and even hints that the economist had half expected such an outcome anyway.

Economics can seem a bit of a mystery. The concepts are simple enough, but they are cloaked in a mystique understood only by high flying financial types or mad-looking academics. The subject is as old as time itself. Noah's forty days in the great flood were seasonally adjusted from sixty seven (due to the poor weather). Hundreds of years later, in 1492, Columbus sailed the Ocean Blue and discovered the world's first tax haven, the Bahamas.

This little guide will admit you to the joys of supply and demand, the rapture of elasticity, and the ecstasy of absolute and comparative advantage. Such knowledge should impress your friends, gain you instant admittance to important places, and seriously improve your love life.

SUPPLY AND DEMAND

The concept at the heart of economics is **supply and demand**. It is its *raison d'être*. Economists would have you believe that there is simply not enough of anything to go round, so that goods and services have to be rationed by attaching prices to them. The balancing of what is available with people's willingness to pay is the essence of supply and demand. If you remember nothing else about economics, you should remember that. Unfortunately that appears to be all most students of economics do remember, having contracted raging narcolepsy by chapter two of the average economics text.

In general, the quantity of any particular product demanded by consumers falls as the price rises. That is to say that if the price of a pint of beer rises, as a rule, people will buy less beer. At the same time the quantity that suppliers wish to supply increases with price as the potential profit rises. So the cheaper something is, the more you will want to buy and the less factory owners will be inclined to produce. So far so good, but it gets better. The price at which supply equals demand is called the **market price**. It is attributed with more mystical powers than a five leaf clover and a leprechaun put together.

Thinking of exceptions and qualifications to the basic supply and demand rule is not difficult and takes us nicely on to some of the finer points of the concept.

Diminishing Returns

Most people understand that it is possible to have too much of a good thing. For example, contrary to popular kindergarten belief, too many chocolate bars can bring on a severe case of **diminishing returns**. This occurs when one chocolate bar is heaven, a second is nice, the third fine, until eventually you could not look at another without being sick. For most products returns are indeed diminishing, with the benefit gained from each additional purchase declining and eventually becoming zero or even negative. An example of this might be the mythical jug of Guinness that never empties, no matter how much is poured from it. What use would a second or a third be apart from starting an international franchise?

Elasticity

Another aspect of supply and demand is **elasticity**. Many people, on discovering that this has nothing to do with frilly underwear, lose interest. However, elasticity does help explain why sales of different goods react differently to changes in price. It measures how sensitive consumers are to changes in price. Demand for such basic goods as bread is said to be price inelastic since the amount of bread bought changes little with price. If the price of a loaf rises, generally consumers have little choice but to pay it. By the same measure, you would have to be very keen on sandwiches to significantly increase bread consumption if the price were to fall.

Luxury goods, by contrast, are often very price elastic. Tea at the Ritz is not considered by most to be one of life's necessities. Consequently if the Ritz's price for a cuppa and cucumber sandwiches rose too much, people might have muffins at home instead.

Other goods, such as Ferraris or caviar, are sold

largely on their 'snob value' or exclusiveness. In such cases some people are prepared to buy more at a higher price.

Some retailers find that certain goods have to have a fancy price before buyers are convinced of their 'quality'. Charge £50 for a weekend for two in Ellesmere Port and you would probably have no takers. However, £500 for a romantic sojourn in Elles Mere Porté might be a different matter. The presentation of such goods is crucial to their appeal. It is for this reason that the leading perfume houses are reluctant to have just anybody selling their 'exclusive' products. It may be quite some time before you see Chanel No. 5 next to the dog food at your local supermarket.

By the same token, gadget freaks will pay anything to be the first in their street to own a solar powered light bulb. As soon as such items become commonplace they lose their appeal.

It is not just consumers who suffer from inelasticity, it also affects the producers. A baker might buy a doughnut-making machine that makes a maximum of 2,000 doughnuts a day. To produce just one extra doughnut would require an extra machine. As a result the baker would produce in multiples of 2,000. If demand rose slightly from 2,000, he is likely to react by raising the price to choke off the extra demand, rather than increasing the output. Bottled spring water merchants could be considered to have a very high production elasticity – after all, how much extra effort does it take to stick an extra plastic bottle under the tap?

The Economic Man and Utility

For simplicity's sake economists are wont to refer to what is known as the **Economic Man** to illustrate the various principles of economics. Although this is both sexist and sad, you, in keeping with hundreds of years of tradition, should do the same. Both the sexism and the sadness pale into insignificance when one considers the plight of any person conceived by a committee of economists.

Economic Man's goal in life is assumed to be to maximise his **utility**. That is, he will consume goods and services in such a combination as to gain the greatest satisfaction from life. Technically utility is defined as the satisfaction derived from the consumption of some good or service. The maxim that 'The best things in life are free' is wasted on him.

Essentially utility explains how and why both companies and individuals make particular economic decisions. Any decisions are made with a view to maximising utility within the budget available.

Marginal Utility

Our Economic Man is having a meal and has to decide whether a chicken biryani or another pint of lager will give him the greater satisfaction. What he probably does not realise is that he is actually making a judgement about **marginal utility**. Theory dictates that he will choose the one that has the highest marginal utility to him. Thus he will opt for the one that adds most to his total satisfaction. However, if he is experiencing diminishing returns from the lager, he might choose a rat vindaloo. In that case the theory of marginal utility has little to do with it.

MONEY

Money is a unit of measurement against which the relative value of various goods and services can be gauged. As a medium of exchange, it allowed people to trade with each other without having to break into a whole bison to buy a box of matches. It is so convenient that life without it, even if you haven't got any, is unthinkable.

At a very early stage traders sought to exchange goods for things that had an innate and recognised value to act as a store of wealth. Gold and other precious stones and metals have been used for centuries, though they are widely felt to have held back the development of the payphone.

Tokens

Some got around the problem of buying matches by rubbing two boy scouts together. Other early civilisations developed the use of small tokens, which could be exchanged for matches. The tokens themselves were pretty worthless, but, within the community in which they were used, they had an understood value. For such a system to work, people using the tokens would have to be confident about three things:

1. That the tokens would be universally accepted.
2. That the supply of the tokens was relatively fixed.
3. That, in the case of chocolate money, some little toe rag would not eat them.

Confidence is what the entire monetary system is based on. Today, more than at any other time in history, money is an act of confidence.

Bank Notes

People accept payment for their labour in small bits of paper that have little or no intrinsic value. The only reason they are prepared to do this is because they know the paper can be used to buy things.

Bank notes derive from 17th century goldsmiths issuing receipts for the gold that people deposited with them for safe keeping. It soon became more convenient, and safer, to use these 'notes' in payment for merchandise, rather than to stagger around with large sums in gold. Thus the ownership of the gold could change without the need for it to be moved from its vault. In the early days everyone was happy to use notes, backed by the promise of a reputable bank to supply the gold they represented, as money. Even to this day British bank notes are inscribed with the legend "I promise to pay the bearer on demand the sum of one pound". This sum was to be paid in gold. Nowadays, bank notes are no longer exchangeable for gold (in fact a £5 note is not exchangeable for very much at all).

Bank Loans

Soon banks, or the goldsmiths who acted as banks, discovered they could actually issue more notes than they had gold deposited in their vaults. Nobody really appeared to mind and it seemed like a 'nice little earner'. In this way the banks could literally create money. If someone wanted a loan, hey presto, your friendly goldsmith could whistle up one of those marvellous notes showing you had a deposit of gold in his safe. The fact that you didn't actually have any gold was academic: you got your loan and the bank got its interest.

Now you do not have to be an Einstein to spot the potential difficulty with this little number. What happens if all the people holding these notes from a certain bank wanted to swap them for gold all at once? Exactly.

Of course, the chances of everyone coincidentally wanting their gold back at the same time are infinitesimally small – perhaps not even that big. However, if depositors should have some reason to lose confidence in the bank, that is another matter. If a bank's largest customer absconded, or fell off a yacht, this could prompt a run on the bank's deposits and, ultimately, bankruptcy.

Bank Regulation

In days of yore, banks collapsed all the time and depositors simply took pot luck. Nowadays such collapses are less common as there are many and varied rules and regulations to ensure the financial integrity of the banks. Even if a bank does go belly-up, deposit insurance means depositors get at least some of their money back.

Money and banking have now virtually come full circle with 'cash' itself becoming an anachronism. The favoured method of payment is once more gold or platinum (banks are still keen to have their products associated with precious metals) – but this time of the plastic variety.

MICRO & MACRO ECONOMICS

When economists speak of **macro** economics they mean looking at the big picture of the economy. That is, taking a view of a whole country or, increasingly, the entire world. It covers the sort of subjects that make newspaper headlines, like unemployment or inflation.

By contrast, **micro** economics is the application of economics to individuals, groups or companies separate from the economy as a whole. It looks at the sort of things you might expect to see if you could look at the economy under a microscope. Thus you could examine how a manufacturer decides where to locate a business, how many people to employ and why anybody bothers making cuckoo Christmas cards – the ones that fold at the top and push all your other cards off the television when they fall flat.

The tenets of micro economics can prove most useful should you ever feel that a discussion is starting to slip away. This might be because you are faced with an advanced bluffer (more commonly known as an expert). However, in such situations there is nothing like inserting a fatuous micro economic theory for regaining the upper hand. The conversation might proceed as follows:

Expert: "Well of course we all know that they are doing their best, but I do believe that the board of XYZ plc hasn't got the faintest idea of where its **production possibility curve** lies."

Bluffer: "Ah well yes... I see, but I really think that it comes back to basic supply and demand and letting the market determine the price."

Expert: "Er…quite. More tea vicar?"

For those who are interested in parrying on a higher level, a production possibility curve shows the set of maximum possible combined outputs of a company producing two (or more) products. Clear? It tells you whether or not a company is producing to its full potential.

A problem with micro economics, and economics in general for that matter, is that theories cannot be tested in the laboratory. This is good news for beagles and fluffy bunnies, but not for the rest of us. It has the unfortunate consequence that silly ideas get that much further in economics than they would normally in the more exact sciences. The Gold Standard is a perfect example of this. It had a superficial appeal to some, but in practice it was a fiasco.

The nearest an economist can get to laboratory conditions is to take a very simple situation and then say what should happen *ceteris paribus* (all other things being equal).

Economists are rather fond of using Latin or French to try to gloss over the subject's shortcomings. Instead of saying that the economy is being allowed to go to the dogs, the government would be said by its economic advisers to be adopting a *laissez-faire* (or non-interference) policy. Of course a *laissez-faire* policy is nothing of the sort. No government in history has ever not meddled in some way. Nonetheless it is quite a useful expression to bear in mind for bluffers with continental inclinations.

If you delve a little deeper into micro economics, you enter a curious world of **internal economies of scale** and **horizontal integration** (most people's favourite). Although simple and fairly harmless, such jargon invariably causes confusion amongst the uninitiated. One word of caution though. If you suspect you have a 'real' economist in your audience, beware. You run the severe risk of being told that your view is fine in theory, but falls down when one considers the **heteroskedasticity** of the production possibility curve over an entire industry. If caught in this way, you have no option but to make a hasty exit muttering something about having left some toast under the grill. The alternative is to be sentenced to an evening nodding sagely as a new-found friend expounds on the joys of adaptive expectations and auto regressive errors.

Micro economics tends to be a rather academic preserve, with the City whiz kid economists preferring the more 'glamorous' macro approach. There is some truth in the rather barbed comment that micro economics is only useful for writing books about micro economics. Much of the subject consists of strictly defining exactly what is meant in economic terms by mundane, everyday words, such as cost and production. However, you would be missing an opportunity if you were totally to ignore micro economics. Simply knowing that economics is based on a flimsy foundation of the patently obvious and old wives' tales will help greatly when jousting with the so-called experts.

UNEMPLOYMENT

This is a robust subject for after-dinner grandiloquence, but needs a little care in the presence of the occupationally challenged (i.e. unemployed). Most people consider unemployment to be the major economic issue of our time. It is far more tangible than a trade deficit and has a devastating impact on those who fall victim to it.

In the 'olden days' unemployment was virtually unknown, mainly because it was very well disguised. In a largely agrarian economy, almost everyone, young or old, would do some manner of work. Even the village idiot would have a role, though quite how this later evolved into town planning is uncertain.

Underemployment

The problem in mainly agricultural communities tended to be underemployment. Large families would try to eke out an existence from a tiny smallholding. It was only after the industrial revolution that the true extent of underemployment was revealed. With the dawning of the industrial age, people left the fields in droves to seek the prosperity of the cities. However, as boom inevitably turned to bust, these people, who had previously been under-occupied in the countryside, became fully unoccupied in the cities. The lack of industrial jobs increased competition for what work was available and drove wages down sharply. With no unemployment benefit people were desperate for work: remember nobody had heard of traffic wardens or encyclopædia salesmen in those days.

Unemployment & Early Economic Theory

The post industrial revolution period was when people first became aware of unemployment as a major social and economic problem. Some of the early theorists argued that if only wages could fall far enough, full employment would somehow inevitably follow. The lowest-paid would simply drop out of the market through malnutrition and death. The rationale for this is straightforward and, at first glance, fairly persuasive. Whilst unemployment remained, there would be downward pressure on wages until such time as wages were low enough to produce full employment.

Keynesian Theory

Between the wars, John Maynard Keynes observed that full employment was anything but typical. Just as today, you didn't need very good eyesight to see that. It was Keynes' contention that the level of consumption and investment decided the level of employment, and that it was only coincidental if full employment resulted. This argument can be bluffed to lethal effect. It is a simple enough statement, but runs counter to normal supply and demand economics, which will confuse those unfamiliar with it.

Essentially Keynes' argument boils down to this bite-sized bluffing chunk: jobs depend on the level of investment and consumption in the economy. If this level is insufficient, it is incumbent on the government, being by far the largest investor and consumer, to put the matter to rights.

Those inclined to the radical, slightly left of centre view of unemployment might want to consider this approach. However, they should be aware that, unless they are tax exiles, such altruism can prove expensive.

So how does all this government investment reduce unemployment? Keynes developed an argument that was first made by a chap called Kahn in the early 1930s. His theory was based on the observation that when people receive extra money, they spend some of it and save the rest. He labelled the proportion of the extra money spent the **marginal propensity to consume** (MPC). However, one man's spending is another man's income. As the first person spends his windfall, so someone else receives extra money, of which they spend a proportion. A major government project, such as building a bridge, benefits the entire community by employing labourers who spend most of their wages locally. The government **kick-starts** economic activity by initiating major projects and allows the impact to ripple outwards. Keynes maintained that governments faced with high unemployment should cut either interest rates or taxes (to aid investment) and initiate investment projects itself. It is a peculiar fact that even the most hard line governments tend to adopt Keynesian policies close to elections.

Marxist Theory

Karl Marx, inveterate leftie and darling of Socialist Workers who never did a day's work in their lives, had a more fatalistic view of unemployment. He argued that for a firm to remain competitive, it would have to employ labour-saving devices. These devices would cut employment and therefore, spread over the whole economy, would reduce demand for the goods being produced. This would necessitate more labour savings, which would cut employment further and leave fewer people in a position to be able to afford the goods being produced. Ultimately this would lead to a calamity marking the end of the capitalist system. Quite simple really, but, fortunately for all the capitalist oppressors amongst us, wrong.

Today's economists have no clearer idea of how to solve unemployment than their forebears. However, to obscure this, they have imbued the subject with jargon. A few choice definitions, therefore, are a useful addition to the aspiring economist's armoury.

Full Employment

What is full employment, you may well ask. Surely it cannot mean literally what it says. It would be unfair to berate the government just because it failed to find a job for your terminally work-shy Uncle Jack. Because of all the technical difficulties with achieving absolutely full employment, the term has been redefined as 'high and stable' employment.

There are various types of unemployment:

1. **Structural unemployment**. This can occur when a particular region of the country is hit by the decline of a major industry. The general level of unemployment therefore reflects deep seated problems within the local economy. Bluffing Note: Blame the government.

2. **Cyclical unemployment**. This arises when the economy is simply suffering from a lack of demand. This is the type of unemployment that occurs in recessions and is expected to decline quickly once the economy picks up. Bluffing Note: Blame the Germans and the Bundesbank.

3. **Frictional unemployment**. This is caused by inefficiencies in the labour market which occur if workers made redundant in one area of the country are not prepared to move to another area where jobs are more plentiful. Bluffing Note: Blame the workers and unions.

4. **Residual unemployment**. This covers those who are to all intents and purposes unemployable. Bluffing Note: It smacks of mocking the afflicted to include politicians and double-glazing sales representatives in this category.

INFLATION

Inflation is probably one of the few really complicated topics in economics. Most other things are made to look hard, but are in fact quite simple. Inflation, however, appears deceptively easy and has baffled economists for decades. This should not be allowed to stand in your way. Just remember that bluffers only have to have an opinion on the subject, however misguided. One would be unfortunate indeed to be actually exposed as such by being made Chancellor of the Exchequer.

Put simply, inflation is the rate of increase of prices. If inflation is 10% per annum, the cost of a $100 basket of shopping would rise to $110 after 12 months. After a further year the cost would rise another 10% to $121.00 and after a third year, it would rise yet another 10% to $133.10. From this, one can begin to see the pernicious effect of compounding. Not only do prices rise every year, but you also see 'inflation on inflation'. Even though inflation may be constant at 10%, the annual price rise becomes ever greater. As can be seen from the shopping basket example, the increase in the first year is $10; in the second year the rise is $11, and by the third year it is $12.10. The important point to make is that even if the rate of inflation falls, prices do not actually go down. A lower rate of inflation translates into a slower rise in prices, not lower prices.

The History of Inflation

For great periods of history inflation was not really an issue. Prices simply did not change all that much. If they did rise, it was usually because some king or other became bored with his courtiers' wives and decided to start a war. Such bellicose activity tended to push up the prices of many basic goods. Henry VIII was less remembered for his tough, anti-inflation budget of 1540 than for his pioneering techniques in the headectomy field. However, in modern times, particularly from the 1960s, inflation has become a veritable monster. It is all the worse because it cannot be seen. It usually strikes late at night when honest folk are in their beds. Before you know it, Fido's dog food is a pound a week dearer and granny needs a mortgage to go to the wrestling.

The absolute dread of inflation is perhaps a little misplaced. This fear was triggered by Germany's inter-war **hyperinflation**. Prices rose out of control and wheelbarrow-loads of money were required even to buy a newspaper. There were even cases of wheelbarrows full of money being stolen with the thief dumping the virtually useless contents. Prices often doubled in an hour. Shop assistants were like hyperactive children on speed trying to update all the prices, and 'shopping around' died a sudden death. Germany's hyperinflation is often used as the reason why all inflation should be eradicated, but many countries have had 100%+ inflation without going hyper.

When there is hyperinflation it is clear that there is little point in trying to save money since it would lose virtually all its value in a matter of hours. It is much more sensible to spend it on something, anything, that will not lose its value so quickly. To a lesser extent the same can be said about normal inflation. If inflation is 20% and interest rates are only 15%, there is little point in 'investing' money in savings accounts. Although the numerical value of your savings would increase by 15% per annum, the purchasing power of each pound would fall by 20% – a net loss of 5%. The real interest rate in this example is said to be -5%, which is the actual interest rate minus the rate of inflation.

The smart thing to do at times of rapid inflation, particularly when the inflation rate is higher than general interest rates, is to borrow money. In such cases, the real value of the loan would be steadily eroded by inflation.

Inflation and House Prices

Mortgages are an especially good example of borrowing money in the hope that inflation will erode the real value of the loan. Many non-bluffers forget that rising house prices are as much a form of inflation as a penny on a loaf of bread.

There have been many periods when wages, prices and, in particular, house prices have risen very rapidly indeed. Although the amount borrowed may initially seem an enormous sum, the real value of the loan will fall sharply after a few years of high inflation. For example, inflation of 10% per annum halves the real value of a mortgage in less than seven years. This is why your parents' mortgage repayments appear tiny compared to your own. Another facet of this type of inflation is that the price of the house rises, creating a capital gain seemingly from nowhere. Explaining house prices in terms of inflation gives one an alternative slant to that perennial dinner party topic. Although this will be of interest to most home owners, you will bore the socks off anyone without a mortgage.

The Downside of Inflation

For those on fixed incomes, such as pensioners, inflation can be a disaster. Inflation erodes their life savings and their pensions steadily lose their purchasing power. Just as inflation can prove a boon to borrowers, it is a deterrent to lenders and investors. In times of high inflation people are discouraged from lending money for fear that its real value will fall. Lenders demand higher rates of interest to compensate for the loss of value whilst the money is being loaned.

In exactly the same way, that rare breed of people who invest in business and industry find that investment returns do not compensate for inflation. They will take their money elsewhere, leaving nobody to fund such worthy products as those little garden windmills with plastic men chopping wood.

Cost-Push and Demand-Pull Inflation

Many attempts have been made to 'cure' inflation without actually determining the real cause and this is usually a fruitful bluffing approach. There are at least two distinct types of inflation, **cost-push** and **demand-pull**. In some cases the two may amount to the same thing, but in others, it would be like mistakenly diagnosing a brain tumour as a headache. If inflation is being caused by increased **OPEC** oil prices, it is unhelpful to rein back consumer demand with high interest rates.

Cost-push inflation occurs when rising costs of production force prices higher. This can happen when wages rise or when the cost of raw materials, such as oil, increases. To maintain profits, producers are then obliged to pass on as much of the cost increase as possible to the their customers.

Demand-pull inflation occurs when demand for a commodity exceeds its supply and producers are forced to increase prices to 'choke off' the excess demand. The mechanism of demand-pull inflation is quite simple. Money grabbing capitalists, faced with greater demand for their products than they can supply, exploit the downtrodden consumer by raising prices. More generally, demand-pull inflation tends to occur when people find that they have more money to spend, say after a tax or mortgage rate cut.

In such cases industry is sometimes unable to meet the sudden upsurge in demand and simply charges as much as people are prepared to pay.

The risk of demand-pull inflation is a fairly eloquent way of arguing against tax cuts if you should wish to do so. There is little point in putting more money in people's pockets if the net effect is simply to push up prices. The UK has a disturbing tendency to only cut taxes when the economy is already booming. The result is that industry does not have the spare capacity to supply all the extra goods which consumers wish to buy, so prices rise. It would make more sense to cut taxes in a recession when industry has plenty of spare capacity, and raise them again in a boom to prevent demand-pull inflation. This seems so obvious it hurts, though judging by some of the world's great leaders it doesn't hurt enough.

Inflation and Unemployment

Economists talk of the 'natural rate of unemployment' – sometimes even more technically defined as **NAIRU**, the non-accelerating inflation rate of unemployment. This is an attempt to define the lowest rate of unemployment achievable without sparking off increased inflation. The interaction between unemployment and inflation is a complex one and is beyond the scope of most economists. However, several have tried to formalise the relationship and bluffers can make a valuable contribution here.

It is commonly assumed that there is some sort of trade-off between unemployment and inflation. This has an intuitive appeal since increased demand can reduce unemployment, but it can also be a cause of inflation. This is the origin of that rather unfortunate phrase 'unemployment is a price worth paying for low inflation'. In 1958 a fellow called Phillips refined the argument somewhat. He defined what has come to be known as the **Phillips curve**. This was a chart showing the interaction between employment and wages or prices. The curve excited feeble-minded politicians because it gave the distinct impression that inflation would fall if the government could tolerate higher unemployment. However, what tended to happen was that inflation improved only temporarily, whilst unemployment ratcheted higher.

Although the theories were widely discredited in the 1970s, they still form the basis of the fight against inflation today. Professor Phillips is also famous for inventing a model of the economy using plastic tubes and coloured water. The model proved extremely useful in promoting employment. It took six plumbers a total of 1,000 hours to stop all the water leaking out.

ECONOMIC GROWTH

Growth is another word which seems fairly straight-forward until economists get their hands on it. A booming economy is easy to spot, but '1% per annum real economic growth' means little more to most people than the average computer bar code.

GDP or GNP?

Economists talk in terms of **GDP** (Gross Domestic Product) or **GNP** (Gross National Product). Bluffers can simply interchange either term for growth in conversation to score vital early points in the "I don't understand it, so they must know what they're talk-ing about" stakes. So what is GDP and does it kill 100% of all known germs?

GDP measures the total level of productive activity in the economy. Thus it measures the total value of all the cars produced, the coal or minerals mined and all the services given during the year. If that total is 1% greater than in the previous year, then economic growth is said to be 1% per annum. However, the value of goods and services, as measured by price, could go up simply due to the effects of inflation. Because of this, economists tend to talk in terms of **real growth**, as if unreal growth meant that buildings appeared as mirages, only to disappear when someone tried to get inside.

Real growth actually takes account of inflation and in economics 'real' anything tends to mean inflation-adjusted. Thus if nominal, or actual, growth is 7% p.a., but inflation is 5% p.a., real growth is only 2% p.a. Just in case someone asks, GNP is broadly the same as GDP except that it also takes into account exports and investments abroad.

Growth and Employment

Economic growth is the key to maintaining employment, but tends to be treated as a secondary objective. This is because voters tend to focus on unemployment or the Prime Minister's hair cut rather than that real GDP was only 2.3% this year.

The Keynesian way of promoting growth is:

1. for the government to reduce interest rates or taxes to encourage investment.

2. for the government itself to get things going by initiating investment programmes.

The more modern view (remembering that there is nothing new in economics) is that if sufficient red tape is removed, growth will be promoted. There is little wrong with this as it stands, but opinions differ widely on what are legitimate areas for deregulation. Simplifying VAT rules is to be applauded, but allowing underage children to sweep up asbestos dust is more questionable.

Measuring Economic Growth

Economists try to measure growth in a number of ways, which in theory should give the same result. The idea is that all the income earned in the economy should equal all the spending in the economy, which in turn should equal all the output in the economy. Therefore it should only be necessary to measure one of them. However, the vagaries of data collection can result in some large discrepancies. Once all these figures have been gleaned, they are then published in booklets, only ever to see the daylight in the *Financial Times* or *Wall Street Journal*. Even the most enthusiastic bluffer would find a telephone directory more interesting.

Unrestricted Economic Growth

Although growth is an important factor in keeping unemployment under control, there are many who question its desirability. Progress at any cost is no longer acceptable and bluffers can show their green credentials by citing environmental factors. Others will point to the ever increasing gap between rich and poor. Despite capitalism's best efforts, modern economics has not been able to reverse the ever widening gulf between the 'haves' and 'have nots'.

During the 1980s many believed that high taxes stifled enterprise amongst high earners to the detriment of the whole economy. To this end, top tax rates were slashed in the expectation that this would have a **trickle-down** effect on the rest of the economy. High earners would earn more, spend more and pass some of their wealth down the economic ladder. The actuality is, as ever, somewhat different to the theory. High earners tend to save a greater proportion of their income than those less fortunate than themselves. As a result there is less left to trickle down. In addition, whatever money they do spend tends to make other high earners even richer, rather than benefiting Joe Public. If the ultimate aim is to improve everyone's lot, it would be better to cut the basic rate of taxation.

Should you ever be asked how growth can be maintained given the world's finite resources, begin with "I'm glad you asked me that question". Go on to explain that the pace of technological innovation is such that goods are being produced more and more efficiently. Computers are an excellent example. It was not so very long ago that a machine the size of Manhattan was required to calculate 2 + 2. Nowadays the task can be accomplished by a pocket calculator (though strangely it now takes forty children and their teacher to achieve the same result with a paper and pencil). But, the real problem, you say, is to ensure that the benefits of growth are spread more evenly. There is much truth in Gandhi's assertion that without greed there would be no shortage.

INTERNATIONAL TRADE

International trade is in essence an extremely simple subject, but unfortunately it touches on the raw nerve of national pride. One can fondly imagine that without French farmers or Japanese car makers, everything would be hunky-dory. This simply is not true. However, if French farmers spent a little more time farming and a little less time spreading manure along the Champs-Elysées, that would be a start.

There are three approaches to world trade.

1. Bash foreigners.

2. Come up with detailed and highly complicated theories that bash foreigners.

3. Take a global view of the situation.

The first approach, although popular with the more functionally illiterate newspapers, is considered a little blunt by most. The third is too sensible by far and too rare to be worth a mention. That leaves number two.

Absolute and Comparative Advantage

The economics of the benefits of world trade essentially revolves around the terms absolute and comparative advantage.

If Japan can make cars more cheaply than the United States, then Japan is said to have an **absolute advantage** in the manufacture of cars. In those simple terms it is clear that Japan should produce cars. By extension, the French should stick to wine, the Germans to beach towels and the British to cunning gadgets for painlessly removing unsightly nasal hair.

What, others may cry, of all those countries which are not very good at producing anything at all? The elegant answer is that each country should concentrate on the product that it produces most cheaply. Thus, even if Japan can make both cars and computers more cheaply than the United States, there is still hope for the latter. In theory it should not be necessary for American car workers to go around smashing up Japanese cars. This is because if either Japan or the United States were to deploy resources to make anything but their respective 'most efficient' products, the available resources would not be used to their maximum potential.

This is where the term **comparative advantage** comes in. Japan may have an absolute advantage in the manufacture of both cars and computers over the United States. However, the United States will have a comparative advantage over Japan in the manufacture of computers if the US is better at producing computers than cars. Of course this is an outrageously simplistic model, but it illustrates that there can be a role for all in international trade. The important point is that every country has a comparative, if not an absolute, advantage over others in something. Therefore, the world will be making the best use of its resources if each country concentrates on what it does best. The Falklands may be a lousy place to breed sheep, but the islanders should still breed them if that is what they do best. There would be little point in them doing something that they are even less good at.

This is a theory that really works, though its effectiveness depends on there being few barriers to trade. The rice trade between Japan and the United States is a case in point. For historical reasons Japan maintains its rice industry despite its production costs being many times those of the US. If Japan was a free market for rice, with no tariffs or subsidies, the money being inefficiently used to produce rice could be switched to cars or computers. These could then be sold to buy cheap rice from the US.

ECONOMIC DATA

You cannot really be expected to make accurate, detailed forecasts of economic data: after all, even highly paid economists fail miserably on that score. However, you can glean much about the current state of affairs by paying a minimum of attention to the newspapers and television. If all is doom and gloom and several acquaintances have just lost their jobs, it is reasonable to say that the economy is still in recession. Likewise, if you see several new cars in your street, either a transporter driver is on his lunch break, or things are picking up.

The official statistics that economists study are usually a month or more out of date, whereas you can deal with the here and now. Harry S. Truman's comment, "It's a recession when your neighbour loses his job; it's a depression when you lose your own", captures the spirit of the bluffer's economic outlook. The secret is to play it as you see it, and only use economic data or press reports when they serve your purpose. Start with a view on the economy and then work everything else around it. Open-mindedness is not considered a virtue among economists.

The following is a brief run through the major economic reports, complete with tips and tactless one-liners.

The Employment Report

The most tangible economic report in any country is the employment report. The figure that grabs the headlines is the unemployment rate – essentially the percentage of people out of work and claiming benefit compared to the total number of people available for work. There are of course plenty of people out of work who, for whatever reason, are ineligible for benefit and they are not counted in the figures.

A slight problem can arise when the figures are **seasonally adjusted**. Just to confuse matters, most countries issue both seasonally and non seasonally adjusted unemployment figures. The reason for the seasonal adjustment is that there are regular patterns in the lay off and the employment of workers. Unemployment rates amongst Father Christmases and Grotto Fairies are usually rather low in December, but rise sharply on December 26th. Seasonally adjusting the unemployment data allows statisticians to strip out these 'blips' and get a much clearer picture of the underlying trend.

Bluffer's note: Avoid suggesting to someone who has just lost their job that, seasonally adjusted, they are not unemployed.

The Trade Report

The trade report is another perennial favourite. English-speaking countries almost invariably report large, and sometimes very large, **trade deficits**, for which news readers save their most serious faces. A trade deficit means that a country has been importing more goods than it has been exporting. This is more commonly called 'living beyond your means'.

In some countries, such as the US and the UK, the deficit in the trade of goods is slightly offset by an **invisible balance**. This does not refer to drug smuggling, and for once it is not just another ploy to massage the figures. So-called **invisible earnings** arise from income earned from abroad by the service sector. This can include insurance, tourism and finance. The billions of dollars, pounds or yen that such industries earn from abroad are called invisible earnings for the simple reason that nothing tangible changes hands. Such earnings are every bit as valid as the money paid for manufactured goods, though that may be of little comfort to unemployed car workers. The very improbability of something called 'invisible', makes it an excellent topic for bluffing. A word of warning though: make sure you remember where you put it down or you'll have a devil of a job finding it again.

In short, the **trade balance** is the value of exported goods minus the value of imported goods. The invisible balance is the difference between payments flowing in from abroad (either as interest or for services rendered) and payments flowing out of a country. Putting these two together you get the **current account**, which gives an overall picture for both goods and services.

The reason trade or current account deficits are such bad things is that they mean a country is not paying its way. In most cases it means that the country is not selling enough cars, tanks and toothbrushes to pay for all the video cameras and computers that its citizens buy from the likes of Japan.

"Does it matter?" you may ask. In the short term the answer has to be "not much". However, longer term, if trade deficits become endemic, a country's currency will become weaker and its standard of living will fall. Bluffers afflicted with weak currencies should express outrage that their government is allowing their currency to be devalued by neglecting economic policy. Your country is being sold short and the dollar, pound or whatever in your pocket is losing its value.

Taking the example of the US (though the same could equally apply to the UK or Australia), a trade deficit means that US citizens are purchasing more foreign currency to buy imported goods than foreigners are purchasing dollars to buy US exports. The simple rules of supply and demand take over. The relative lack of demand for the dollar forces its price (the exchange rate) lower, so that a dollar will buy fewer foreign goods. It is for this reason that prices in well-run countries like Germany and Japan seem so expensive to the British and Australians. Years of trade deficits erode the value of a currency and leave its citizens poorer than countries which pay their way.

Bluffer's note: It is a universal truth that rich countries run trade surpluses, whilst poor countries have deficits. The only reason a rich country runs a trade deficit is if it is on the way to becoming a poor one.

The Inflation Report

This is usually referred to when making pay claims. Every month most countries survey the prices of a wide range of consumer goods and services. The figures are then manipulated into a price index. Dividing the current month's index by the index number for the same month a year earlier produces the so-called **annual rate of inflation**. One of the highest annual rates of inflation in recent history is the 25.5% seen in the UK in the third quarter of 1975, in the wake of the 1973 'oil shock'. Typically UK inflation tends to run at between 3% and 10% with 10%+ usually spurring the government into action and sub 3% bringing on a severe case of complacency. The major difference between Britain and Germany has got nothing to do with beach towels, it is that Germany regards 3% inflation as being too high.

Bluffer's note: Since the causes of inflation are very little understood, you can usually play things one of two ways depending on your political allegiance:

1. Refer to cost-push inflation, blaming international factors such as oil price shocks
2. Blame domestic factors and government mismanagement (demand-pull).

Either way, don't forget that inflation is often referred to as a hidden tax. However, unlike conventional taxes, it is somewhat more difficult to fiddle.

The Budget Deficit/Surplus

This is the one that tax cuts are supposed to hang on. If a country is running a **budget deficit**, it means that government tax receipts and other income undershoot government spending. This shortfall generally has to be made up by the government borrowing money. Typically it will do this by issuing a bond. The bond states that the bearer will be paid a regular rate of interest for the life of the bond and will then receive his/her money back at the end of the loan. In theory, if the government is already borrowing a lot of money, tax cuts are a bad idea, though try telling that to a government in an election year.

The national budget is unfortunately a subject that has been rather hijacked by those who equate running a country with housekeeping. They believe that to borrow any money is to live beyond one's means and so is intrinsically bad. This is just simple enough for backbench members of parliament to understand. However, if ever there was a subject where a little knowledge is a dangerous thing, this is it. This is why governments try desperately to cut spending in the middle of a slump, exacerbating the recession. The mistake is then compounded by cutting taxes just when the economy is already growing too fast. As a result, inflation rises and so too do interest rates and the **boom bust cycle** starts all over again.

Bluffer's note: Despite all the hot air, tax cuts have nothing to do with the state of the economy and little to do with the budget deficit. If a country can afford to cut taxes it probably does not need to, and if it needs to it almost certainly cannot afford to.

A SHORT ECONOMIC HISTORY

It is most effective to have a suitably impressive historical example to support whatever otherwise preposterous view one may be espousing. There are countless instances to choose from and most can be used to support either side of the same argument. It is fun to mix and match and, with practice, it is possible to move seamlessly from one unfortunate episode to the next without ever getting to the point.

The Black Death (1346-50) – A Study of Money Supply and Inflation.

Bubonic plague swept into Europe from the Far East in 1346 and killed approximately 75 million people. However, as is usual when faced with a major human tragedy, the economists of the day fretted about the money supply. The upshot of this catastrophe was that the amount of physical coinage in the economy remained roughly the same, while the quantity of goods being produced, rather understandably, fell dramatically. With the same amount of money chasing fewer goods, prices rose sharply, a phenomenon called inflation.

Inflation is often thought of as a fairly modern concept, only arising to a significant degree in the late 1960s. However, in England prices rose over 30% in 1351 as Europe finally started to shake off the Black Death. The concern about rising prices even brought about one of the very earliest forms of incomes policies when the Statute of Labourers was introduced in a vain attempt to freeze wages. Thus you can say, with some justification, that there is nothing new under the sun in economics. You can even lament that numerous so-called 'modern policies' have a track record of failure over many centuries.

If you should catch the plague, trade union membership might prove more useful than a doctor. That way you would have funds to pay for your funeral.

The Devaluing of Henry VIII (1542)

King Henry VIII was famous for having got through six wives, but is less well known for his skills in currency devaluation. Today devaluation is often seen as a way of compensating for a country's loss of competitiveness. Thus, if wage rises are too great and production costs are too high, the simple solution is to devalue your currency. This will reduce the price of your exports in terms of marks or yen, making them more competitive. At the same time the cost of your imports will rise and choke off the demand for them. However in old Henry's time international trade was in its infancy and the key purpose of devaluing was to finance his debt.

The King was fond of travelling abroad to bash foreign heads together, but it did tend to cost rather a lot of money. Consequently he often ran severely into debt though, strangely for a man with so many ex-wives, he paid very little alimony. His cunning plan was to make the debt payable in pounds, whilst his reserves were largely in gold and silver. If his debt rose too much, he would simply issue a decree raising the price of gold and silver and effectively reduce the value of the debt.

The moral is: never trust a fat man with a beard (and a cod piece) asking for a loan.

All Big Bubbles Burst (1720)

The year 1720 was a bad year for speculative bubbles: two of the most famous, the Mississippi and the South Sea, burst. A speculative bubble occurs when people become obsessed with a particular investment. Fear plays a large part in the bubble's build-up, with investors desperate not to 'miss the boat' and willing to buy at any price, completely disregarding logic. Fraud is often involved; and the old adage, that a fool and his money are easily parted, was as true in the 18th century as it is today.

The Mississippi Company held a monopoly on all French territories in North America. The King of France and the French government were enthralled by the prospect of the untold riches promised from the New World. They allowed the Royal Bank to issue bank notes backed, not by gold or silver as was common at the time, but by shares in the Mississippi company. When the company crashed in 1720, the entire French monetary system was wiped out. Even people who had not invested in the company lost out as the bank notes became worthless. To this day the events of 1720 explain French monetary caution, though not why they cannot produce a decent rock band.

Britain was spared a similar fate when the South Sea bubble burst, but only just. These are only the most illustrious of many such bubbles, with investors at various times whipped into a frenzy over sugar, canals and even tulip bulbs. You can draw a modern day parallel with the collapse of the Japanese property market in the early 1990s. Land prices fell by well over 50% in Tokyo and a multitude of financial institutions crashed, often fraudulently.

Remember that being wise after the event is both the economists' and bluffers' stock in trade, so fire away. The more outrageous, the better.

The moral is: if something seems too good to be true, it is usually illegal.

The Wall Street Crash (1929)

The Great Crash is widely, and falsely, blamed for precipitating the 1930s depression. What it actually did was lay bare the fragility of the world economy. In less than three years US stocks lost almost 90% of their value and did not regain their pre-crash levels until the mid-1950s. As ever, the cause was an unbridled speculative frenzy. The US economy had been recovering nicely from the 1920-22 recession and profits rose correspondingly.

Everyone imagined this could go on for ever and investors frantically bought shares, borrowing huge amounts of money to do so. One wag at the time commented that 'the present level of stock prices discounts not just the future, but the hereafter'. The thing to do in such cases is to nod sagely and recall past examples, saying that it will all end in tears.

If you really want to impress, you can blame the US Federal Reserve Bank, the central bank responsible for setting interest rates. It was too slow to increase interest rates to choke off the speculative frenzy and then raised them just as the crash struck, thus compounding the error.

A sure sign that things have moved beyond the pale is when people start borrowing money to gamble on the stock markets.

The Great Depression (1930s)

There are several misconceptions about the Great Depression. The popular image is of tumble-weed blowing through 'Dust Bowl' towns all but obliterated by financial collapse and drought. However, whilst unemployment did reach 25% in some of the major economic powers at the time, this still meant that 75% of people had jobs, and in general, their standards of living improved considerably. The 1930s was actually a period of innovation and development with such inventions as the electron microscope, the television, the tape recorder and, more ominously, the rocket.

What the Depression did do was to convince policy-makers that the deflationary economic policies peddled by classical economists did not work. Classical economics is a hotch-potch collection of early economic theories which amount to prescribing public expenditure and wage cuts as the cure for all economic ills.

You could draw a rather compelling parallel with early doctors who would recommend a course of leeches for every ailment from the common cold to cholera. Try to resist the temptation to strangle anyone who suggests arbitrary cuts in public spending as a cure for economic depression. In a debate, resorting to violence, though gratifying, tends to weaken your argument.

The Gold Standard (RIP 1936)

Here you are talking about economic folklore. Just as many East European communists pine for the glory days of the Cold War, some dyed in the wool economists still urge a return to pegging foreign exchange rates to the value of gold. The basic idea was that a country could only issue paper money in proportion to the quantity of gold it held in its reserves. This harks back to the origins of bank notes, which started out as receipts for deposits of gold. It may help to think of it as a kind of economic fundamentalism. The gold standard effectively fixed foreign exchange rates between countries on the standard, which prevented countries from devaluing their way back to competitiveness if wages rose too much. This all sounds harmless enough, laudable even, but the rub was that the system could not cope with a major depression.

Under the gold standard a country's trade deficit was financed by exporting the requisite amount of gold to balance the accounts. In 1925 the pound was ludicrously overvalued, which made British exports hopelessly uncompetitive. As Britain's gold reserves fell, the supply of money was reduced in a vain attempt to restore competitiveness by forcing prices and wages down. However, all that was achieved was to nail the economy to the floor. Wages simply could not be reduced far enough to make British exports competitive (in part due to rising union power). Thus Britain had to continue to export gold to balance its trading account. In 1931, its government gave up the unequal struggle. The United States survived until 1933 before succumbing. In characteristically obstinate fashion the Belgians continued until 1935 and the French until 1936, both at an horrendous cost to their respective economies. The parallels between the gold standard and European Monetary Union are striking and are worth pursuing vigorously.

Remember that the only certainties in life are death, taxes and the fact that slavishly following economic dogmas always ends in catastrophe.

The Marshall Plan (1947)

At the mention of the Marshall Plan you can allow yourself an approving sigh. You can then reflect that the plan enjoyed a rare, if not unique, distinction amongst economic plans in that it was a tremendous success. After World War II, Europe was on the brink of economic and political collapse. The Continent was so chronically short of money that it could not afford its own reconstruction. US Secretary of State General George Catlett Marshall overcame the handicap of his middle name to put together an extraordinarily far-sighted aid package. The US made available huge credits for reconstruction and development and gave European exporters privileged access to American markets. Marshall Aid was even offered to the Soviet Union, which did the economic equivalent of looking a gift horse in the mouth.

The programme included a not insignificant 'gift' of $17 billion from the US to Europe as well as credits from the newly formed **World Bank**. Marshall Aid played an important part in mitigating political discontent in Europe and fostered an atmosphere of political and strategic cooperation amongst the western nations. The Plan's creator was awarded the Nobel Peace Prize in 1953. It says something about economists that he never won the Economics Prize.

Bretton Woods and All That Jazz (1944-71)

The foundations of a new world order for international finance and trade were laid at an historic meeting at Bretton Woods in New Hampshire, USA in 1944. The **IMF** arose from the meeting with the object of working towards free trade at stable exchange rates, whilst the World Bank was charged with providing credit for reconstruction and development. Around the same time **GATT** was created with the express aim of keeping down barriers to free world trade.

The Bretton Woods agreement introduced a new regime for managing global currencies, more flexible than the gold standard, but not as chaotic as allowing currencies to vary at the whim of the financial markets. The aim of all this activity was to avoid the economic failures of the inter-war years and to that extent it, like the Marshall Plan, was a dramatic success.

However, praising successes is not really what economics is all about. In 1971, after the dollar had become increasingly over-valued, the Bretton Woods system of semi-fixed currencies collapsed. The moral is: there is no such thing as a cure-all in economics.

The Oil Shock (1973)

The Arabs got a bit of bad press on this one. The bare facts are that oil prices quadrupled when the oil-producing nations restricted the supply of oil during the 1973 war with Israel. Prices also soared in 1979 after **OPEC** went for an encore. However, the war can only be regarded as the pretext for the price rises, rather than the fundamental cause. Oil was, and still is, priced in dollars on the international markets.

The break up of the Bretton Woods system of semi-fixed currencies in 1971 had led to a severe devaluation of the dollar. This in turn sharply reduced OPEC's oil revenues. Thus, although the US may have gained a short term competitive advantage from the dollar's devaluation, everyone paid the price.

The moral is: what goes around, comes around.

The 1987 Stock Market Crash

For all the similarities between the 1929 and 1987 stock market crashes, there are one or two vital differences. The most important of these was the reaction of the financial authorities. In 1929, the US Federal Reserve reacted to the crash by raising interest rates, effectively clamping down on credit. This caused many otherwise healthy companies to fail simply due to cash flow problems. If one company failed leaving debts, many others down the line would meet the same fate.

In 1987 the authorities were quick to lower interest rates and to ensure that ample credit was made available to help institutions overcome their difficulties. There were no widespread business failures and, more importantly, the economy did not enter another depression. There was a period of recession (milder than a 1930s-style depression), but this was largely due to a resurgence of inflation. The sharp interest rate cuts, and excessively hasty financial deregulation, pushed inflation higher, which in turn forced governments to reverse earlier interest rate cuts, prompting an economic slow-down.

The immediate cause of the crash is unclear. Some blame Germany's Bundesbank for bursting the bubble by raising interest rates. Others blame the financial markets, questioning how a share could halve in value overnight when nothing had happened to the company or its markets. The essential point to make is that, once again, greed had overtaken logic. People continued to buy shares because they thought that the price would continue to rise indefinitely. Eventually the market became top heavy with people investing borrowed funds.

If you borrow money to invest, you lose money you have not got as soon as share prices start to fall. This is what happened in 1987. Once the slide started, many leveraged investors (the ones who had borrowed) were forced to sell their shares rapidly in the face of escalating losses. The fall in share prices turned into panic selling on a global scale from Tokyo to New York. As world stock markets collapsed in 1987, government bonds, which pay a guaranteed, fixed income, saw unprecedented panic buying. You can use this example to underline the point that one should never put all one's eggs in one basket.

The clear warning here is that whenever you feel you must buy something for fear of 'missing out', take a deep breath, and go and mow the lawn.

The ERM (Good riddance, 1992)

Like the gold standard before it, the ERM became the panacea for every economic woe. By tying Europe's multifarious currencies together it was envisaged that European union, and a single European currency, would miraculously emerge from the chrysalis. Freed from the uncertainties of currency movements, the economies of Europe would be able to reap the benefits of closer cooperation and more open markets. Just think about that next time all flights to Majorca are cancelled by Spanish air traffic control.

Should you encounter a little too much 'Euro enthusiasm' for your tastes, you have a number of options.

The most effective of these is to highlight the impracticalities of merging a well-run country like Germany with a governmental disaster such as Greece. The key point about currency weakness is that it is a symptom of an economy's problems rather than the cause. The pound and the lira are usually described as weak currencies for several very good reasons, not just at the whim of merciless foreign investors. They are weak because, at any one time, Britain and Italy have some or all of the following problems: high inflation, heavy government borrowing and a burgeoning trade deficit.

This may sound a little harsh, but bluffers are not supposed to have feelings. There is no place for the rose-tinted glasses of patriotism in the cut and thrust of the financial markets. In short, trying to coordinate currencies, rather than economic policy, is like trying to cure a fever by putting the thermometer in an ice bucket.

The Barings Collapse (1995)

One of London's oldest banks, Barings was once described as the sixth major power in the world behind Britain and France. It was brought to its knees after losing more than its entire net worth trading derivatives.

In its most basic form, a derivative is a contract that gives an investor an opportunity or an obligation to buy or sell something for a fixed price at some future date. The risk comes from the fact that no money changes hands when the deal is struck and only the net profit or loss is settled on the trade. Thus enormous bets can be taken on the financial markets with little or no capital.

For weeks traders were aware that Barings had a huge losing bet on Japanese derivatives. However, just as nobody on the Titanic shouted "Mind that iceberg!", nobody imagined that Barings was not in control. When the crunch came, everyone pleaded ignorance. A scapegoat was duly found and a sugar daddy saved everyone's bonuses.

After "When should I buy my holiday money?", the next most commonly asked question of anyone with a vaguely financial bent is "What are derivatives?". The best answer is that they are "highly geared financial instruments that enable investors to both hedge and speculate at relatively little initial outlay". It is usually advisable to move the conversation rapidly to something a little easier, like the Theory of Relativity.

Economic history shows one thing above all else: that the more things change, the more they stay the same. Many seemingly unrelated events are in fact related and, as far as economic disasters are concerned, history certainly does repeat itself. You can set your watch by Mexico's currency crises (once a decade at last reckoning). Earthquakes in Japan will periodically rock the world economy, and it is unlikely that Bre-X's 'goldless' gold mine in Indonesia will the last of the genre. There is no calamity so great that it has not happened before and will not happen again.

Feel free to link seemingly disparate events together at will. Not only is it fun, but you might actually come up with something.

LEADING NAMES

When it comes to the leading names in economics, the task of who to recommend as 'sound' is tricky. A cruel, but ultimately fair joke at economists' expense runs as follows:

Q: What are the similarities between economists and ties?
A: Neither serve any useful purpose, but no self-respecting businessman would be seen dead without either.

To judge by the results of their policies, there would seem to be a dearth of real economic talent. So instead, here is a quick run down of some of the better known personalities.

Milton Friedman

Chicago University's Milton Friedman is perhaps the best known monetarist in the world, but probably the name least likely to impress your audience. His 1980s book and television series *Free to Choose* met with somewhat less than ecstatic critical acclaim. His work was an attempt to persuade us that there were no circumstances in which legal or government intervention in the markets was justified. He argued that regulations to ensure consumer safety from dangerous goods were unnecessary in a perfect market. His rationale was that a manufacturer would be deterred from producing such goods by the bad publicity that would result from a defect. After all, would you buy another parachute from someone who had just sold you a dud?

John Kenneth Galbraith

Galbraith is probably the most widely-respected economist alive today. His books sell well and his ideas are logically and wittily presented. Other economists may have won Nobel prizes, but JKG as he is known to those who have never met him, has combined popular credibility with the real role in top level policy formation in the United States. How much more perfect can a role model get?

John Maynard Keynes

Keynes is one of the most famous figures in economics. By all accounts a man of immense intellect, he moved easily in the circles of the Bloomsbury Set and the great thinkers of his time. His heyday was the inter-war period and his key contribution came in 1936: a most worthy book called *The General Theory of Employment, Interest and Money*.

Apart from having an eye for a catchy title, Keynes was also passionately opposed to the classical theories, which seemed to advocate **deflation** as the answer to everything. Keynes maintained that employment depended on the level of investment and consumption in the economy. He said that if unemployment was too high, the answer was to increase government investment and expenditure. This was diametrically opposed to the classical view, which held that high unemployment could be countered by cutting wages. Keynes favoured judicious **intervention** at times of high unemployment. By contrast, the **monetarist** policies, of using high interest rates and cutting government expenditure, exacerbate such situations.

It is this intervention aspect that is right at the

heart of the clash of economic ideologies. Opponents of government interference, particularly those of an entrepreneurial bent, feel they are being discouraged from endeavour by punitive tax rates and red tape. But who likes paying taxes?

Adam Smith

Adam Smith is the grand-daddy of modern economics. Use the word 'modern' advisedly since his seminal work, *The Wealth of Nations*, was published in 1776. Smith's book is a rambling affair and not in the least bit funny.

At times the great man strayed well outside the area of what would now be regarded as legitimate fields of economic study. He did however set out the basics of economics as they were understood at the time and provided a framework upon which the subject could be developed. His common sense, free-market way of thinking survives today and forms the basis of classical economics. His approach is encapsulated by his view that "What is prudence in the conduct of every private family can scarce be folly in that of a great Kingdom". You can safely blame him for the failure of countless governments over the centuries to take action to alleviate privation and hardship through public investment.

Karl Marx

Marx is something of a maverick amongst the great and the good in the field of economics. The quip "What can you expect of a communist?" can be expertly brushed aside by pointing out that Marx's ideas were simply adopted by the Soviets, rather than dreamt up specifically for them. His theories, though now widely discredited, were at times inspired. He was virtually the first economist to acknowledge the issue of unemployment. However, it is his thoughts on the capitalist system that he is best remembered for.

Marx's argument against capitalism was essentially quite simple. In brief, he prophesied that the capitalist system would collapse under its own weight, unable to consume all the goods it produced. **Thomas Malthus** originally claimed exactly the opposite, that the population would grow geometrically to absorb resources which increased arithmetically, before being persuaded otherwise. Keynes described Malthus' change of heart as 'a disaster to the progress of economics'. Others might regard anything which hindered the progress of economics as something of a blessing.

Other economists of note include: **Friedrich August von Hayek**, an Austrian who won the Nobel Economics Prize in 1974, 30 years after the publication of his celebrated book *The Road to Serfdom*, and whose free-market views came back into fashion in the Reagan/Thatcher years of the 1970s-1980s; **Max Weber**, German sociologist and political economist who, in *The Protestant Ethic and The Spirit of Capitalism* (1904-5), challenged Marx's theory that economic factors are decisive in determining the course of history, and **Alan Greenspan**, three-term Chairman of the U.S. Federal Reserve Bank (who is yet to receive full credit for an unprecedented period of high growth and low inflation during the 1990s), and who is too busy getting it right to write a book about it.

SO WHAT WOULD YOU DO?

To Control the Economy

This is the rub. You have an economy to run, perhaps the most intricate mechanism known to man, and you have just two levers to control it with. These levers are obscurely called 'fiscal and monetary policy'. For the purposes of bluffing, and/or running the country, fiscal policy is all about taxation, whilst monetary policy involves fiddling with interest rates. Outrageously simplistic, but there you are.

In essence the options you have are fourfold: to raise or lower taxes, and to raise or lower interest rates. (A word to the wise: policy makers never actually 'raise' taxes or 'increase' interest rates, they 'tighten fiscal policy' or 'apply the monetary brake'.) It's pretty much like driving a car with a brake and accelerator, but no steering wheel. For good measure, you get several million backseat drivers thrown in.

Taking the car analogy a little further, and given the very limited means of control, it would stand to reason that the levers should be handled delicately. Don't you believe it. Sparked into action by a mid-term dip in the opinion polls or impending elections, most governments first cut taxes and then apply the turbo by lowering interest rates as well.

If you were in charge, you could find yourself in a similar position. Everything might be going fine when an unexpected political scandal throws your government into disarray and prompts a rash tax cut. Thus an economy that was cruising nicely is suddenly thrown off at the first curve as you put your foot to the metal. The country spins helplessly towards economic oblivion as you fight valiantly with the limited controls.

You slam on the monetary brakes, raising interest rates sharply. The economy finally comes to a recessionary halt, but you still have to find the money to pay for the tax cut that you made when your ratings took a dive. So, just when the economy could do with some help, you have little choice but to apply the fiscal handbrake by raising taxes. Strangely, governments rarely do this by reversing the particular tax cut that caused the problem in the first place.

Such economic cycles happen with pathetic regularity all over the world and are entirely self-inflicted. Our elders and betters would have us believe that they are protecting us from the ravages of an uncertain global economy. However, the indisputable line to maintain is that major shocks and surprises are not the way to run a school tuck shop, let alone a major world economy.

To Assess the Economic Outlook

This is ideal territory for the bluffer. The very essence of bluffing is to bamboozle everyone into thinking you know what you are talking about. Yet with economic policy a modicum of common sense is all that one needs. Rather than having to weave a web of pretension, you will probably find that most people will agree with any moderately sensible idea you espouse.

Use your intuition to tell you what is happening to the economy and don't be afraid to draw your own conclusions. If you order a maternity dress and the shop tells you it will take nine months to deliver, this tells you something about the economy. It suggests that the factory is already working flat out and so, most likely, are its competitors. Thus it would be folly to suggest the need to increase consumer demand

further by cutting taxes and lowering interest rates –
even though this is what happens time after time. On
the other hand, when high street shops are offering
large discounts and immediate delivery (the dress not
the baby), you may confidently proclaim that tax
increases are unlikely to be required.

To Formulate Economic Policy

The conundrum you will face in common with most
world leaders is that it is tempting to try to achieve
two or more diametrically opposed economic objectives at the same time. For example, you may try to
lower inflation *and* unemployment. The problem is
that the sort of policies that reduce unemployment
usually increase prices (and vice versa). The net
result is that prices still rise and the jobless total
climbs by at least one as you are voted out of office.

Achieving the multifarious objectives of economic
policy-making (high growth, zero unemployment,
minimal borrowing and low inflation) can be likened
to that infuriating game with a number of tiny silver
balls that have to be manoeuvred into various shal-
low holes. Getting one or two balls into holes is no
problem at all, but filling all the holes simultaneously
is next to impossible.

Usually governments get round this by setting
themselves one overriding objective, for example, to
reduce inflation. You will do the same. Thus blink-
ered, you set about your task with missionary zeal,
brooking no opposition from either your colleagues or
the country at large. Very often you will be successful
in the narrowest sense of the word, but with cata-
strophic consequences. In 1979 the US and UK govern-

ments simultaneously decided to tackle inflation with aggressively tight monetary policy (i.e. penal interest rates). The US prime rate (the rate at which US banks lend money to each other) rose to 21% in 1980. The result, particularly in the UK, was that inflation dipped temporarily, whilst unemployment rose permanently. Nice one.

The most popular, and least successful, policy is 'fire fighting' where the government lurches from one crisis to another in a never ending state of agitation. A more considered approach is to entrust control of such things as interest rates to an independent third party, such a central bank, which is increasingly common, but by no means universal. In this way the direct link between politics and economic policy is weakened and, in theory, there should be more continuity and certainty about policy.

All the major economies of the world have central banks. They can be regarded as the government's own bank. They will commonly be responsible for issuing bank notes, raising loans to finance government spending and protecting the nation's currency.

Virtually all of the world's central banks set interest rates in their respective countries, but many only act on the orders of their masters in the government. The choice would be yours. Germany's Bundesbank is regarded as the most independent, and successful, central bank. Although appointments to the Bundesbank's Directorate do have to be rubber stamped by the government, politicians recognise that undue interference would do more harm than good. Consequently the Germans tend to have the lowest interest rates, the strongest currency and own all the best property in Europe.

In the US, the Federal Reserve Bank is also nominally independent, but appointments tend to be more overtly political. Even so, the US President would have to find a very good reason for not reappointing a 'Fed' Chairman who appears to be performing satisfactorily. What tends to happen is that Fed Governors, once appointed, go 'native' and become far less subject to political pressure.

In New Zealand the central bank president's annual bonus is determined by how successful the bank has been in reaching its inflation target. If this sounds tempting, ask yourself whether you'd like your monetary policy conducted from an old VW camper van.

To Compare Your Performance

In theory it should be possible to compare the performance of different countries by looking at the official data published by each of them. However, in practice, this is not always possible. In the 1980s the UK altered the method of calculating unemployment almost 30 times. Amazingly, none of the successive new measures actually increased the jobless total. Some suspect that every time a French satellite is launched it is counted as an export. This would make their trade report about as useful as a wet baguette.

As ever, the best comparisons do not come from official sources. A long-time favourite has been the Big Mac Index which compares the cost (converted into US dollars) of the burger in the major nations. As a rule, the countries with the strongest currencies tend to have the most expensive burgers. You might not appreciate having your economic performance assessed on the basis of the price of a Big Mac, but it has the merit of actually working.

Another 'popular' indication of global prices is known as the Moët Luxury Index. It measures increases in the dollar prices of such things as Rolls-Royce Corniche IV convertibles, men's Rolex Oysters and a round trip Concorde flight between Paris and New York. A bit closer to home is the Misery Index, which simply adds together the rate of unemployment and the rate of inflation.

It is said to move inversely to the stock market. The awful truth is that it is very difficult, if not impossible, for government policy to make a positive contribution to the economy. The best that can be hoped for is that your actions do not cause too much damage.

Real governments are advised by legions of economists yet still make mistakes, so a healthy scepticism of economists and their prognostications is in order. If you ask someone how the economy should be run and they produce pages of equations, it is the surest sign in the world that they haven't got a clue, but wouldn't mind having a go. Have-a-go-heroes may be fine in fighting street crime, but when it's the economy that is being mugged that is a different matter.

The beauty of economics is that you don't need to be able to derive an econometric model from first principles. Being a boffin only seems to deprive you of the common sense approach that is essential to good bluffing. The trick is to stick to things that can't easily be disproved within the memory span of your average dinner party guest. This is why economists are so confident sounding off on television about their long term forecasts, but are far more reticent predicting what the dollar's value will be in half an hour's time. So using your eyes and ears and, most importantly, your intuition, credibility is a breeze.

GLOSSARY

Boom bust cycle – The 'wheel of fate' phenomenon whereby an economic boom seems to be inevitably followed by a bust.

Budget deficit – What happens when a government spends more money than it receives (mainly through taxation).

Bundesbank – The Central Bank of Germany, rather like the Bank of England, but a bit more independent. There is little truth in the rumour that its board eats live babies for breakfast, though it has been known to sacrifice the odd country.

Classical economics – A way of referring to early economic theory, much of which remains in use today since so-called 'modern' economists cannot agree on what to replace it with.

Current account – The excess of exported goods and services and net interest received by a country over imported goods and services. Boring and important in equal measures.

Deflation – Vicious circle whereby falling income levels reduce consumer demand, which reduces income still further, and so on.

Depression – The economic equivalent of the psychiatric condition.

EMU – European Monetary Union. An idea set in process by the Maastricht Treaties of 1992. Many valid comparisons have been made between this and the famous flightless bird.

ERM – Exchange Rate Mechanism. Sad league table

of European currencies from which the pound and lira were unceremoniously dumped in 1992.

GATT – General Agreement on Tariffs and Trade. An international trade accord signed with great fanfare agreeing to reduce trade tariffs to the levels prevailing when the talks began.

Heteroskedasticity – A regression disturbance caused by the lack of homogeneity amongst the statistical observations. Serves you right for looking.

IMF – The ubiquitous International Monetary Fund. The loan sharks of international finance. When countries screw up, it is to the IMF that they turn. The *quid pro quo* is that the IMF insists on ruinous economic policies to restore 'prosperity'.

Internal economies of scale – Cost benefits derived as a firm becomes bigger, such as being able to order paper clips in bulk. An **external economy of scale** results from the growth of an entire industry. If the industry is big enough, it might be worth someone's while to build a really big paper clip factory to reduce the unit cost for everyone.

Intervention – Interference from the government, or any other official body, in the workings of the markets. Publicly owned airlines of the world (Iberia, etc.) are tragic examples of tax payers' money being flushed down the pan.

Kick start – Fanciful idea that the economy can be sparked into life in the same manner as a motorbike.

MPC – Marginal Propensity to Consume. Measure of the proportion of any increase in income which would be spent (as opposed to being saved). If you are anything like us, it will be 100%.

Monetarist – Adherent to an economic policy based upon the control of the money supply, via interest rates, to reduce inflation.

Official interest rates – The rates at which banks can borrow money from the local central bank. Known in the UK as 'the base rate'; 'discount rate' in most other countries.

OPEC – The Organisation of Petroleum Exporting Countries. One of the world's more successful cartels.

Phillips curve – Graph showing the alleged trade-off between unemployment and inflation.

Production possibility curve – Graph showing the optimum output combinations for a given company.

Real interest rate – Rate of interest minus the rate of inflation. 'Real' anything in economics means that it has been 'adjusted' for inflation.

Real growth – See above.

Seasonally adjusted figures – Statistics which have been 'adjusted' to take account of seasonal factors, such as the increased demand for balls during Wimbledon fortnight.

Trickle-down effect – Process by which policies making the rich richer are supposed to benefit everyone in the economy.

World Bank – International bank capitalised by the world's major countries to finance development projects. Neat idea, but it is generally agreed that zillion dollar hydroelectric dams are possibly not the best solution to famine and poverty.

THE AUTHOR

Afflicted by Welshness since birth, Stuart Trow now lives in exile with his wife and orientates his life around the 6.31 to London's Liverpool Street Station.

A keen athlete, his achievements on the rugby field never quite matched his enthusiasm, so he was left with little choice but to become an economist.

At the LSE the subject of his seminal work was the economics of the rock music industry. The height of his rebelliousness these days is to avoid the *Financial Times* whenever possible, except when it publishes a letter from him or one of his cronies.

He began work in the city moments before the 1987 stock market crash, though nothing was ever proved. Since then he has worked for a succession of little-known companies. Most recently he joined Japan's Norinchukin Bank, one of the biggest banks in the world, only to find that no-one had heard of it either.

THE BLUFFER'S GUIDES™

Available at £1.99*, £2.50• and £2.99:

Accountancy
Advertising
Archaeology
Astrology & Fortune Telling*
Ballet*
Bluffing
Champagne•
Chess•
The Classics
Computers
Consultancy
Cricket
Doctoring
Economics
The European Union
The Flight Deck
Golf
The Internet
Jazz
Law
Management
Marketing
Men
Music

The Occult*
Opera
Paris•
Personal Finance
Philosophy
Photography*
Public Speaking
Publishing*
The Quantum Universe
The Races•
The Rock Business
Rugby
Science
Secretaries•
Seduction
Sex
Skiing
Small Business
Stocks & Shares
Tax
Teaching
University
Whisky
Wine

All these books are available at your local bookshop or newsagent, or by post or telephone from: B.B.C.S., P.O.Box 941, Hull HU1 3VQ. (24 hour Telephone Credit Card Line: 01482 224626)

Please add the following for postage charges: UK (& BFPO) Orders: £1.00 for the first book & 50p for each additional book up to a maximum of £2.50; Overseas (& Eire) Orders: £2.00 for the first book, £1.00 for the second & 50p for each additional book.